DISASTER READY TINA:

Fire Safety Procedure

Written and Illustrated by

Edgar C. Reed

COPYWRITE 2014,

By

Edgar C Reed

POB 50296

Fort Myers, FL 33994

ISBN-13: 978-0991534302

ISBN-10: 0991534301

All rights reserved, including the rights to reproduce this book, or portions thereof, in any form whatsoever. No part of this book may be reproduced or transmitted in any form or by any means, electronic or mechanical, including photocopying, recording, or by any information storage and retrieval system, without the written permission of the publisher, except where permitted by law.

TABLE OF TOPICS

1. FIRE SAFETY
2. RACE
3. PASS
4. QUIZ
5. DRILL INSTRUCTIONS
6. ANSWERS

WORDS OF WISDOM

"Nothing in the world exists unless it is imagined. It will exist as long as you hold its image in the mind. When it is forgotten it goes back to nothing in the abyss of the mind."

- Edgar Reed

WORDS OF WISDOM

Imagination is more important than knowledge. It is imagination that gives birth to knowledge. [1]

- Albert Einstein

DEDICATION

This book is dedicated to my sisters Tina and Sharon, my brother Edwin, all my kids, and all my grandkids.

IMPORTANCE OF PLAY PRETENDING

Play pretend or practicing safety exercises in the way of Fire Drills can help you remember what to do when you need to do it. You just use your mind to imagine what you will do if in a fire situation and do it. Soon it will become natural to you as breathing air.

FIRE SAFETY

Disaster Ready Tina says, she has a lesson today that is about Fire Safety Procedure. Tina want everyone to know that mean old nasty fire can destroy, and she would like all kids to be proactive as well as reactive to prevent or reduce the damage fire can cause. Tina says, being a proactive kid is convincing Mom and Dad to install smoke detectors throughout the home, and having an ABC type portable fire extinguisher for every room, and making sure everyone knows what to do if there ever is an actual fire in the home. Being reactive says

Tina, means knowing how to react in a fire situation. And kids can be reactive with pretend play where they would demonstrate to Mom and Dad that they can perform RACE and PASS procedure correctly without them prompting.

RACE

Kids this acronym is a life saver, it can save yours and the life of others. Using RACE will prompt you to remember what to do when a fire threatens your life and property.[2] The first letter "R" prompts you to first, rescue those in danger of being burned by the fire. Remember "R" comes first. The second letter "A" will prompt you to next, alert family in the house of the fire, and then dial 911 to report the fire. The third letter "C" will prompt you to next, close doors and windows to reduce air to the fire and reduce smoke and fumes. The last letter "E" in RACE is a prompt to grab that ABC portable fire extinguisher and try to fight the fire if it is small enough (you be the judge). The letter "E" also is a prompt to you to evacuate or get out of the house and wait for the Fireman to show up and fight the fire. On a side note, the ABC extinguisher is good for the home. It is for trash, wood, paper, liquid, and electrical fires.

PASS

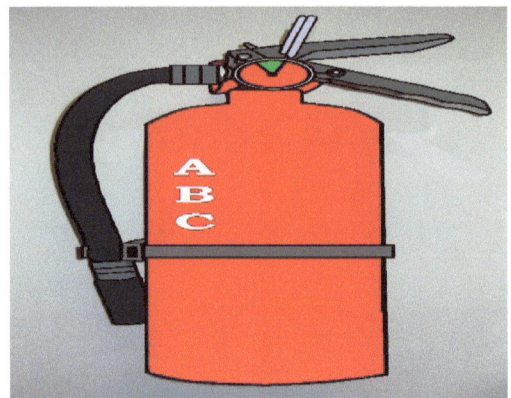

The PASS acronym is good because it helps us to remember how to use that ABC portable fire extinguisher. You want to be sure to perform the series of actions in the order of the acronym (pull, aim, squeeze, and sweep).[3] The first letter "P" prompts you to first, pull the pin at the top of the extinguisher so as to free up the extinguisher trigger to squeeze. The second letter "A" prompts you to next, aim nozzle of the fire extinguisher at the middle or base of the fire. The third letter "S" prompts you to next, squeeze the trigger allowing the chemical agent inside the fire extinguisher to come out.

The fourth and last letter of the acronym PASS is again "S" and it is a prompt to sweep the nozzle of the fire extinguisher that you should have pointed at the base of the fire in a side to side motion.

Let's Play Pretend There Is A Fire in the Home
(Tina's Fire drill)

Step # 1 - Pick an area in the home to place a red colored cone for the imaginary fire.

Step # 2 - Everyone participating in the fire drill goes over RACE and PASS procedure.

Step # 3 - Have everyone go to an area of the home and pretend they are sleeping.

Step # 4 - Begin the fire drill.

Step # 5 - Start drill by performing steps in the acronym RACE.

Step # 6 - Rescue everyone by waking them up.

Step # 7 - Alarm everyone as you wake them by telling them of the fire.

Step # 8 - Alarm fire fighters by play pretend dialing 911 to report the fire.

Step # 9 – Close doors and windows to the area of the fire to delay spread of fire.

Step # 10 – Make determination if fire is small enough for you to fight it, if not get out of home and wait for fire fighters.

Step # 11 – If fire is small enough that you feel you can fight the fire, grab fire extinguisher and use the PASS acronym to help you use the extinguisher.

Step # 12 – Play pretend pulling the pin, aiming the nozzle of the fire extinguisher at the play pretend fire, squeezing the trigger of the extinguisher, and sweeping the nozzle in a side to side motion at the play pretend fire.

Step # 13 – Practice evacuating the home and meeting up together in a designated area to make sure everyone is out of the home.

End the fire drill

Quiz

1. The acronym RACE helps you to remember what to do when there is a fire.

A = True
B = False

2. The acronym PASS helps you to remember how to use a fire extinguisher.

A = True

B = False

3. Smoke detectors alerts use of a possible fire.

A = True

B = False

4. You should dial 911 to report a fire.

A = True

B = False

5. An ABC fire extinguisher is good for fighting what type of fire?

A = Trash, wood, and paper
B = Liquid
C = Electrical
D = All of the above

6. What does "R" in the acronym RACE means?

A = Remove
B = Rescue
C = Run

D = None of the above

7. What does "A" in the acronym RACE means?

A = Activate

B = Action

C = Alarm

D = None of the above

8. We alarm there is a fire in two ways, alert everyone in the house and dial 911 to report the fire to the fire department.

A = True

B = False

Note: Each correct answer is worth 12.5 points.

ANSWERS

1. a
2. a
3. a
4. a
5. d
6. b
7. c
8. a

What was your score on the test?

WRITE DOWN EMEREGENCY PHONE NUMBERS.

Police:

_____

Fire Dept.:

_____

Ambulance:

_____

WRITE DOWN YOUR HOME ADDRESS

Street Number:

_____

Street Name:

_____

City Name:

_____

REFERENCES

1. Herweck, D. (2009). Albert Einstein and his theory of relativity. Mankato, MN: Compass Point Books.

2. Motacki, K., & Burke, K. (2013). Nursing Delegation and Management of Patient Care. St. Louis, MO: Mosby Elsevier.

3. Dougherty, C., & Emigh, R. (2001). The ESL Safety Book. Lewiston, NY: FB Productions.

The author thanks you for your purchase of this safety material.

www.ingramcontent.com/pod-product-compliance
Lightning Source LLC
Chambersburg PA
CBHW041745040426
42444CB00004B/183